Written by Sue Graves
Illustrated by Alison Atkins (John Martin & Artists)
Designed by Blue Sunflower Creative

Language consultant: Betty Root

This is a Parragon book
First published in 2003

Parragon
Queen Street House
4 Queen Street
Bath, BA1 1HE, UK

ISBN 1-40540-053-6
Printed in China

Gold Stars

Noisy Train

A Level 2 Reading Book

p

Notes for Parents

Reading with your child is an enjoyable and rewarding experience. These **Gold Stars** reading books encourage and support children who are learning to read.

There are four different levels of reading book in the series. Within each level, the books can be read in any order. The steps between the levels are deliberately small because it is so important, at this early stage, for children to succeed. Success creates confidence.

Starting to read

Start by reading the book aloud to your child, taking time to talk about the pictures. This will help your child to see that pictures often give clues about the story.

Over a period of time, try to read the same book several times so that your child becomes familiar with the story and the words and phrases. Gradually your child will want to read the book aloud with you. It helps to run your finger under the words as you say them.

Occasionally, stop and encourage your child to continue reading aloud without you. Join in again when your child needs help. This is the next step towards helping your child become an independent reader.

Finally, your child will be ready to read alone. Listen carefully to your child and give plenty of praise. Remember to make reading an enjoyable experience.

Using your Gold Stars stickers

You can use the **Gold Stars** stickers at the back of the book as a reward for effort as well as achievement. Learning to read is an exciting challenge for every child.

Remember these four important stages:

- Read the story **to** your child.
- Read the story **with** your child.
- Encourage your child to read **to you**.
- Listen to your child read **alone**.

This is Noisy Train.
Noisy Train is very noisy.

He likes to blow his whistle.
"Toot, toot!"

He likes to blow it very loudly!

Every day Noisy Train
saw Sheep.

"Toot, toot!" said Noisy Train.
"Hello, Sheep!"

Every day Sheep got cross.

"Baa, baa!" said Sheep.
"What a noisy train!"

Every day Noisy Train saw Sheepdog.

"Toot, toot!" said Noisy Train. "Hello, Sheepdog!"

Every day Sheepdog got cross.

"Woof, woof!" said Sheepdog.
"What a noisy train!"

Sheep and Sheepdog went to see Noisy Train.

"You are too noisy," they said. "Stop blowing your whistle."

Noisy Train was sad.

"I'll stop blowing my whistle," he said.

The next day, Noisy Train saw Sheep.

But he didn't blow his whistle.

Sheep was pleased.

"Baa, baa!" she said.
"That's better."

Then Noisy Train saw Sheepdog.

But he didn't blow his whistle.

Sheepdog was pleased.

"Woof, woof!" he said. "That's better."

But then Noisy Train saw the lambs.

The lambs were on the track.

"The lambs must be moved," said Noisy Train. "I must get Sheep and Sheepdog."

Noisy Train flashed his lights.
"Flash, flash!"

He puffed out steam.
"Puff, puff!"

But Sheep and Sheepdog did not come.

"I will have to blow my whistle," said Noisy Train. "Then Sheep and Sheepdog will come."

Noisy Train blew his whistle. "Toot, toot!" He blew it very loudly.

Sheep and Sheepdog came running. They got the lambs to move off the track.

“Baa, baa!” said Sheep. “Woof, woof!” said Sheepdog. “We’re glad you are a noisy train!”

Read these words. Look back in the book and find the words.

Noisy Train

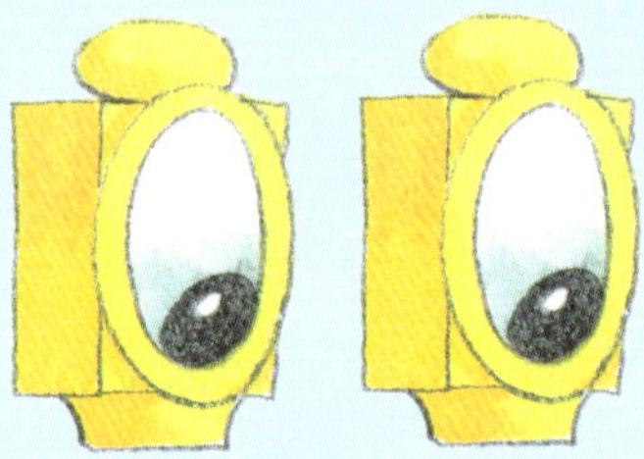

lights

Sheep

Sheepdog

lambs

track

Gold Stars

Level 2 reading books are for children who can recognize simple words and phrases.

- Familiar, repeated phrases
- Short sentences
- Large, clear type
- Fun vocabulary repeated in the pictures
- Word review activity